bringing my words to light

Copyright © 2020 by Afroz Martino

All rights reserved. No part of this publication may be reproduced, distributed, or transmitted in any form or by any means, including photocopying, recording, or other electronic or mechanical methods, without the prior written permission of the publisher, except in the case of brief quotations embodied in critical reviews and certain other noncommercial uses permitted by copyright law.

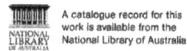
A catalogue record for this work is available from the National Library of Australia

Martino, Afroz *(Author)*
Bringing My Words to Light
ISBN 978-1-922452-91-7
Mr Eaves XL Mod OT Font 10/12

Cover photo by Jasmin Martino
Cover and book design by Green Hill Publishing

bringing my words to light

AFROZ MARTINO

Introduction

I have always wanted to be a writer, to write wonderful stories, poetry, my utmost inner thoughts, and feelings, but I could never find the words. Words do not come to me easily. Occasionally I get a glimpse of the words I want to write, but then they disappear and hide in a dark place where I cannot find them.

For years I was too occupied with caring for my family and friends and I never made time for myself. My husband and daughters have encouraged me to do something. For me. After a long time, I started painting and writing poetry again. Poetry is helping me to understand myself, my relationships with others and try to make better sense of my world.

Today, wherever I look, I see sadness, sickness, racism, violence, and war in the world. People starving and homeless in every city. Natural disasters have intensified due to human impact and the climate crisis. Humans have not learned from their past; we knowingly kill each other and destroy our earth. We must find a way to stop hurting each other and take better care of our earth.

People with disability, people of colour, and women still suffer oppression to this day. I see their struggle to survive and succeed. I see people being treated unjustly. I see vulnerable children walking our streets, lost in their own world, looking for someone or something to love. They only want a place, where they can feel safe and call their home. They are not the only ones. As a human race, we should all treat each other with love and respect.

Despite this, I still see so much beauty in our world. I see the colours of the rainbow, birds flying in the evening sky, and I hear the roaring sound of waves crashing against our shores. I am surrounded by the love of my family and friends.

I see random acts of kindness and a sense of community unity that makes me believe we have hope for peace. We all must contribute to bring peace to our beautiful world.

Social Isolation during the COVID-19 has given me the chance to piece together this book. Writing these poems has given me a sense of belonging and an understanding of being a woman in this world. I want to share my world through my eyes using my words with my family, friends, and people.

I hope you enjoy this book as much as I have enjoyed capturing beautiful words to write these poems.

I wish to express my gratitude and thanks to all those who contributed to this work. I dedicate this book to my husband David and daughters.

My husband, David: who has supported me from the beginning, without him there would be no book.

My four daughters: who have been my source of joy and have given me the strength to face any challenge. My daughters are my greatest achievement.

Lastly, my parents and in-laws who have shown me how to live my life with hope, courage, and strength.

Love you all,

Afroz

let me be me.

Hey Mama, don't you know,
I am trapped between a time in between two lines.
I am happy here, I am just fine.
Just let me be me.

Listen to me Mama, hear me cry.
Let me be me, let me be me.

My lonely heart is lost in a world full of grief,
Please Mama don't ask me to give up
the only friend I have.

Listen to me Mama, listen to my plea.
Let me be me, let me be me.

You took me away from my kin,
You took me away from my nest,
You took me to a place you thought would be best.

Listen to me Mama, I will tell you again.
Let me be me, let me be me.

My new home gave me things,
To feed my body and mind,
But the food for my soul, I could never find.
Please Mama, let me be me.

You wanted me to be just like you,
Which I could never be,
Because I am not you, I am me.

You tried your best, in a land that was not your home,
And I do understand where you were coming from.

But mama I can't be you, let me be me.
I will always love you, but just listen to me.
I want to be me.

let me be me.

My Daughter

Today I saw my daughter cry
and my heart broke into two.
I wish I could hold her in my arms
And tell her this is nothing new.

Cry my daughter cry,
cry until your tears are dry,
Because no one will understand you,
even if they try.

I saw you as a little girl
and not as an adult daughter,
I wanted to tell you that this will pass,
and you will be stronger than ever.

Life is just a journey and you will learn a lot,
But you being a woman and a mother,
an honour please forget not.

I beg you my daughter that you will stand tall,
In the battle of life when many will fall.

You have your children, as I had mine,
You will watch them grow and you will be fine.

In the end, all I want to say is get up and go,
I am your mother and I love you so.

My Daughter

Hey Women!

Dedicated to women going through menopause.

Listen to your heart,
Feel your touch.

Why did you grow up?

Hear your laughter,
Dance in the rain.

Why did you stop?

The stream of life flows within,
Heart still dancing.

Why is there a cloud?

Thunder, rain and hail,
In a mysterious land.

Why can't you see the sunshine?
New road ahead with mist and fog.

What can be found?

Seek out the woman you will be,
Not the one that we left behind.

Hey Women!

Eva my Granddaughter

Our ray of sunshine,
Lightning in the stormy night.

You came into our lives,
Multiplied our happiness and made,
Our days bright.

Your sparkling eyes observe us,
Never missing a single turn.
Fearless in nature and curious of mind,
Copying us as you learn.

Watching you grow older,
Every day on the screen.
I love you and miss you so much,
Waiting to see you soon.

Our hearts break every time you leave for home,
It is not goodbye, it is farewell,
Until we meet again.

Eva my Granddaughter

My Grandson, Aston

If only you knew how much I love and miss you,
My heart aches to see you – I do not know what to do.

Sitting by my window watching autumn leaves fall,
As grey clouds glide above, I am waiting for your call.

You came into my life and changed,
My world.
Then you flew across the ocean and left me in the cold.

Each morning a flock of birds flies over my shack.
Every time, I beg them to bring you back.

You ran and played chase on Nonno's little farm,
I sang you many lullabies as you slept in my arms.

I long for the day I will see you again,
My grandson.
We will laugh. We will cry. We will have such fun.

Alicia

Alicia is our hero, she's champion of the world,
She swam for Australia and brought home a gold.

Alicia is our girl, she's one who always tries,
She never gives up, never stops, and almost never cries.

She swims for Special Olympics, she swims for Arks as well,
She plays netball and that's not all, no, there's still more to tell.

She loves to eat and loves to cook,
But can't be bothered with a book.
Expert with puzzles, Facebook, phones –
What other talents, yet unknown?

Alicia was born different. How she wanted to belong!
Friends came with time –
Alicia had to wait, but she was strong.

Now able friends all have grown and gone,
Is our Alicia left alone?
No! Special sports clubs, new true friends,
And new skills too, our girl has gained.

I struggle to express just what Alicia means to me.
Because of her, the 'me' I am is the best me I can be.

Specialists said you'd never walk,
Specialist said you'd never talk,
But, my child, you've worked hard, and long,
And you're all right, and they were wrong.

Alicia

Sister of Mine

This poem written with love, in twenty-two lines,
Will let the world know how wonderful you are, sister of mine.

When you were an infant, you held your mother's hand,
But soon you found yourself alone in an unfamiliar land.

I travelled through my childhood with you by my side,
We clutched at string while we slept at night.

While drowning in my tears, in you I saw no fear,
Voices from our hearts that nobody seemed to hear.

We travelled across the ocean and made Australia our home,
We found ourselves in adulthood. We laughed, we had fun.

You planted your gardens with fruit and flowers,
You watered them day and night. In all seasons, in all hours.

You won most of your battles but lost a few.
You fight for justice, this is nothing New.

You are my sister, you are my friend,
We will travel and explore until we meet our end.

I loved you yesterday and I love you now,
I will love you tomorrow and
As we grow old.

Thank you for being part of my life, sister of mine.
I dedicate to you these twenty-two lines.

White Bird

My white bird, you flew across the mountain,
blue ocean and white sand.
You brought us a leaf from your land
and dropped it in my hand.

The leaf was perfect for our puzzle, it made us free.
The leaf was the missing link from our family tree.

My white bird brought distance near
and made our journey clear.
Gave us knowledge we do not have for unknown fear.

The leaves knew each other like brothers in this mystique world.
They found each other again and again, together they swirled.

Fallen leaves from the tree, pains like no other.
Found comfort in a foreign land with his brother.

My white bird when it's time for you to fly back home,
Take our pain and take our tears and take our names.

May we meet again in a distant, far away plane,
But now let us live on this infinite terrain.

White Bird

SAKTE is Strength

Five letters in SAKTE written on this page,
SAKTE are the five friends who never seem to age.

Five young women crossed paths in a strange land,
They formed a group, then friendship and an everlasting band.

S is for SERENA, SAVIOUR of the troops,
A is for AFROZ, most ACTIVE in the group.

K is for KATRINA, KNOWLEDGEABLE and keen,
T is for TINGU, where TALENT can be seen.

E is for EVELYN, the most ELEGANT one of all,

This is how they found the name,
SAKTE which they call.

Five friends sitting side by side,
There is laughter and tears as the years go by.
Through thick and thin, lose or win,
Their SAKTE will never die.

1980's

2019

SAKTE is Strength

The Tree

Why are you calling my name and knocking on the door?

I am no one. I am a tree living on a moor.

Why are you looking at me with barely disguised tears?

I am no one. I am the shadow that walks
among the trees with strange fears.

Are you not a daughter?

Are you not a flower that blossomed one fine summers day?

Yes, that was me.

Are you not a wife?

Are you not a tree that stood strong, next to your love,
and weathered many storms?

Yes, that was me.

Are you not a mother?

Are you not a tree that blossoms
 in spring and withers in autumn?

Yes, that was me.

Are you not a grandmother?

Are you not a tree that has brought joy throughout the year?

Yes, that was me.

My dear, do you still believe you are no one?

A tree who lives on a moor.

The Tree

Gift

This little poem was written in 1987.

This poem is dedicated to young lovers. Do not fear to love someone who is from a different culture, religion, colour, class, sex, or ability. We are all special in our own way. Only love and respect can unite us as one nation on earth.

We are one in the spirit,
We are one in the soul,
We are part of each other.
Together, we are one.

We are one in our strength,
We are one in our powers,
We are loved by our God,
And God's blessing is ours.

We can cross any ocean,
We can win any war,
We can travel through darkness,
Cross desert and moor.

Our love is a gift from God,
Given to us from heaven.
How can it be bad or so wrong?
While love stays one and strong.

Gift

Eight days

Dedicated to my late father
Dr. A K M Amzad Hossain Mian

You took eight days to die,
We had plenty of time to say goodbye.
I have no place and I am not able to cry,
Because I cannot, and my eyes are still dry.

With so much pain, you have gone.
We sat by your side, but nothing could be done.

You had dementia; you had many strokes.
There was no cure and no medical hope.

For eight days, you were given no food and water.
We prayed and hoped, but God did not
Make you better.

We watched you suffer; but it made us tougher.
Wish we could have done something,
But we could do nothing.

The memory of your stare is floating in my eyes –
My heavy heart is still not very wise.

I felt what you were trying to say,
I could not find a way.
I thought of putting a pillow on your face,
No one could do it if they were in my place.

I wish I could have taken your pain away.
The things I could have done, I think about every day.

So much anger in my heart,
I don't know how to stop,
To put the anger aside,
But the anger cannot hide.

We lost part of you years before,
But we still could see a glimpse of you sometimes at your door.

This time you have gone for good,
From us and from this world.
For eight days, we sat by your side,
We watched you die, and there was nowhere to hide.

Miss you, my Abba; miss you, my Dad.
No more pain for you; I am so glad.
I wish no one had to go through those eight days,
Our pain and our tears will remain with us always.

My heart feels heavy with so much pain,
I will not say goodbye because I will see you again.

Eight days

Visit

I am dedicating this poem to my mother, Firoza.

Bangladesh, Bangladesh, where I was born,
Bangladesh, Bangladesh, you were my first home.

Memories from that time are held strong in my heart.
I remember much but don't know where to start.

If I stop to look back, what do I see?
Children playing barefoot; one of them was me.

The birds sang until the evening breeze.
We played under a canopy made of old mango trees.

One minute I was playing; the next, I was gone.
We had left the land, we had moved on.

Across the oceans, beyond what you can see.
For 50 years, in this new home, were my parents and me.

Loved ones were lost; life changed night and day.
I longed to go back, but fear kept me away.

Back after 35 years – to see my family and first home,
Back to Bangladesh, with heartfelt tears.

New houses had been built; old ones were gone.
Loved ones had passed away,
everything else remained the same.

The morning sun had risen again, with crisp,
cool air that smelled the same.
The fragrance of jasmine all around,
sparkling dew on the ground.

Chickens running around the yard, cows chewing on hay.

Children playing barefoot,
Brought memories of happy days.

The trees stood as before.
I could hear their rustling song.
'Welcome home,' they said, 'where you belong.'

This is where my story started; this is where I am from.
I am so glad Bangladesh is where I was born.

Bangladesh, Bangladesh, you are a country
of wonders, trees, forests and hills.
Home of the Bengal tigers, creating many more thrills.

Your Padma, Meghna and Jamuna
rivers flow through your land.
For richer or poorer, in sickness and in health,
you are a country grand.

Bloodshed

Sadness in my heart as I watch the evening news.
Murder and bloodshed,
Orphan numbers rising,
And many tears shed.

When they grow up, they will have their revenge,
The cycle of killing must stop – a huge challenge.

I don't understand why they kill innocence.
I don't understand all this violence.

The killing must stop.

With all the knowledge we've acquired, killing is not fine.
I don't have all the answers, but I know that love must shine.
Please help me to understand: why do you want to kill?

I don't know your story, and I don't know your pain,
But in the murder of innocence, there is nothing to gain.

It only makes the hatred stronger.
Can you not see this is wrong?

The cost of winning a battle or war,
Violence begets violence – there will be more.

You could end your hatred by talking,
And end the violence by walking.

We could change this together by trying.
There's no need for all of this dying.

One of You.

When I walk alone in the street,
Please don't judge me, I'm not the only one you'll meet.

Don't call me 'bogan', don't make fun of me.
I am more than what you see.

We are strangers – I don't know you.
There are some who know me, but only few.

You're not in my shoes.
About my past and present, you have no clue.

I've not received any breaks in this life.
It seems I am in constant strife.

My mother abandoned me when I was seven.
I lived with my grandparents and thought it was heaven.

Grandma took care of me; a home, she provided.
Grandpa abused me and called it 'love'.

Grandma could do nothing about the abuse.
I tried to escape, but it was no use.

I had to leave school; I was developmentally delayed.
I studied so hard but couldn't make the grade.

Finally, I ran away.
Life was hard; I had nowhere to stay.

In this shitty life, men walked through the door.
They gave me love and children – not one but four.

Three girls and one boy – they were taken from me.
The Government took them away, as you can see.

I couldn't keep my children happy and safe.
It is so sad – this is the story of my life.

Because of my birth, my children had to pay.
I live this miserable life – what can I say?

I go to sleep every night with a broken heart.
Keep asking myself why I was not very smart.
My wish is for no one to have a life like mine.
You see, dear stranger, I am not fine.

I don't need your pity, nor your abuse.
A little empathy and kindness, I know I could use.

But if you abuse me, it is nothing new.
Remember, dear stranger, I am a person – just like you.

COVID-19

COVID-19 is a virus that came to get us all.
If we don't work together, many nations will fall.

On the 11th of March 2020, the world was told
COVID-19 is a pandemic that kills young and old.

Every hundred years a pandemic is found.
In 1918, the Spanish Flu was around.
Killed 50 million people all over the world.
It seems like nature's way of fighting to balance the Earth.

Fire, cyclone, drought and flood; causing chaos in our land.
All we needed was COVID-19 to give nature a hand.

Believers believe that COVID-19 is God's wrath
Because mankind is not following the right path.

Some also believe we made our earth very sick.
COVID-19 will cause our earth to heal, and it will be quick.
COVID-19 came from China, spreading across, taking lives,
Massive deaths, no hospital beds, fears around, no one is safe.

Lockdown was placed, by March, upon all of us.
Many people agreed, many turned away in disgust.

Social distancing and isolation were created
To stop the virus from spreading.
People stayed home, and everything was closed.

The only places people could go:
shopping for food and medicine.
While the world was looking for a vaccine.

People started doing things slightly differently,
By changing their lifestyles very gently.

They found new ways of living in their homes.
They used social media for their fun.
It made their connections with family better,
And some of them wrote poems or letters.

People could not eat out, so they cooked their meals.
Some of them got no meals because they had to pay bills.

Some had jobs, and some had none.
Some had families who died all alone.

People are dying from hunger and thirst,
Poverty-stricken countries felt its strain first.

Massive deaths all around the world
I wish this COVID-19 would just go away.
We must live with this virus for now and tomorrow,
All waiting for the vaccine; what else can I say?

We have no vaccine for COVID-19.
Without a vaccine, we are not going to win.

This is our new tomorrow, this is our new flame.
We all know things will never be the same.

My Children

Children of mine, I love you so.
You will leave your nest, and you will go.

You will find new ground to build your own little world.
You will create precious stories, which close to you, you will hold.

But take your past with memories of us,
Your Mum and Dad.
Be proud of who you are, and it is not so bad.

Italian and Bengali seeds are planted on Australian soil.
You have blossomed into beautiful people – we have done well.

You are Australian, and this is where you were born.
Take care of your country: this is your home.

My Children

Desperate Snapper

I am a desperate snapper; I swam from very far.
I came to find you by following the bright star.

Please save our home, only if you try.
Do you hear the ocean's shout for help and my children's cry?

My ocean is sick, and my family is dying,
If you think you are safe, you are lying.

You live on land, and I live in the sea –
It is the same world and how beautiful it can be.

Stop harming the world for your greed.
Everything you want, there is no need.
Your kind is the only animal that kills for fun.
What will you do when we are all gone?

Desperate Snapper

Selina

Selina was the name of my maternal grandmother,
We dedicated this name to our third daughter.

Selina is for elegant, lovable, intelligent, nice and admirable.
Selina can be sweet, silly and also sensible.

She is the moon on the cloudy night,
Among the stars, she can also shine bright.

She is like a volcano, which can erupt anytime.
She is nice and cool in the meantime.

She is full of surprises and a little eccentric.
She is very neat and also a clean freak.

She has the cutest smile, with a dimple on her cheek.
She is not only clever but also knows how to speak.

Selina was my challenge as one of my daughters.
I will be born again and again to be her mother.

Goodbye

Before saying goodbye, I want to tell you my sad story,
How I died, in my lover's hand, it was not necessary.

I was full of life and I was in love,
Everything I had, to him I freely gave.

He swept me off my feet and took me many places,
I became wary of him when I discovered
he was a man of many faces.
He started getting angry at me, after a while.
Then he started hitting me,
and he made me feel not worthwhile.

He really felt remorse when he calmed down,
He kept crying and saying, without me his life cannot go on.
He said he loved me and will not hurt me again,
He broke his promise and hurt me again and again.

He kept telling me that he does care,
He was mentally ill; I was not aware.
When I realized that he was extremely sick,
I was not prepared and was not very quick.

I should have left him when he started hitting me,
I could not do it, because he would not let me be free.
I was mortified and I was threatened,
I could not tell because I was frightened.

One day his anger went too far,
As I laid dead in a pool of blood, it was all noticeably clear.

So, my friends listen to my plea,
Please leave this love in a count of three.
First time you will forgive, second time too.
Third time say goodbye and Goodluck to you.

My Autumn

Two little birds sit on a naked branch
watching me as I walk by,
White, wispy, fluffy clouds drifting slowly
across the misty blue sky.

Autumn is here, Autumn is here,
these are the whispers that I hear.

The leaves are falling from the trees,
green, orange, yellow, red and brown.
These are the colours of Autumn leaves,
falling down, will be all gone.

The wind is blowing on the branches
as she is singing her gentle tune,
Making the Autumn leaves swirl and
dance, something to be seen.

Autumn is here, Autumn is here, these
are the whispers that I hear.

Autumn has brought its bright colours,
a sprinkle of rain and the cool breeze,
I feel the rain and the wind against my
face, finding a little peace.

I can hear my name being whispered
by the bare standing trees.
'Afroz dear, we are here, our leaves are not really gone,
They will nourish us from the ground,
the circle of life will go on.'

Autumn is here, Autumn is here, these
are the whispers that I hear.

My Autumn

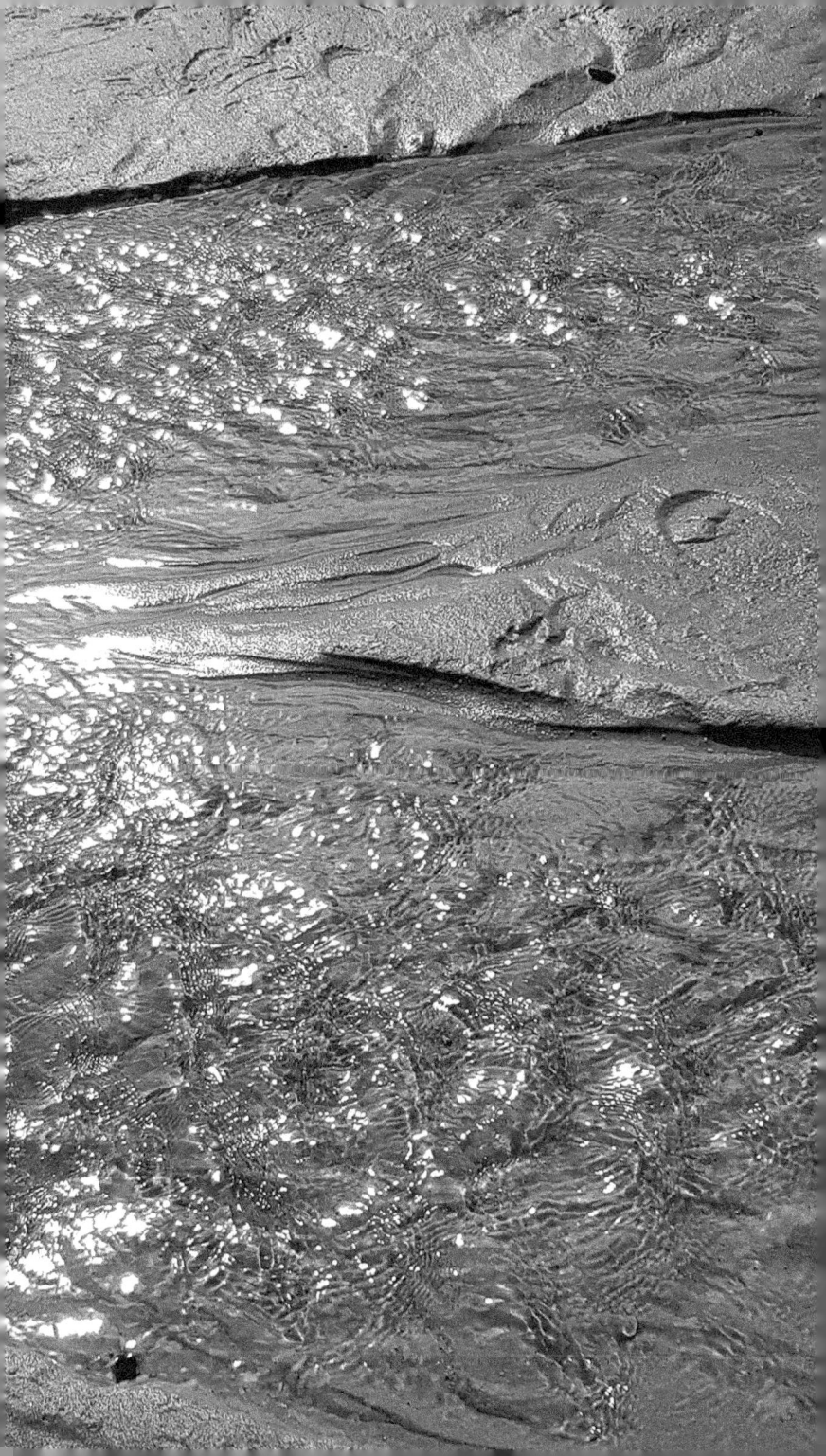

About Me

My name is Afroz Martino and I, along with my younger sister Azmiri Mian, was born in Pabna, a small town in East Pakistan (now called Bangladesh). I am the eldest daughter of Dr A.K.M Amzad Hossain Mian and Firoza Hosneara. As a child I was given the nickname 'Swapna' – the Bengali word for dream.

My maternal grandmother, Selina Begum (Nani), raised me as my mother was only 17 years old when she gave birth to me. My father, an archaeologist, worked a lot and frequently left for excavations in other cities. My maternal side of the family emigrated to Bangladesh from Afghanistan and Persia. My paternal side is more confusing. I was told that they were also migrants from Persia, but later in life we discovered that we also have Greek blood in us. We learnt that my father and sister both have thalassemia-a genetically inherited disorder common in the Mediterranean, but rare for Bangladeshi.

In 1970, my father was awarded a scholarship by the Pakistani government to study for a PhD in Greece; he left that year, and we joined him later that same year. While living in Greece, my mother almost died from an ectopic pregnancy.

While this was happening, a war broke out between Pakistan and East Pakistan. My father's scholarship from the Pakistani government ceased, and with no income to continue the PhD or feed the family, we were asked to return home. My father wanted to stay in Greece and continue his PhD and, luckily, was granted a scholarship by the Greek government. However, the scholarship money was not enough to support the family, so my mother and I started working in a clothing factory.

Every morning I had to get up early to go to work, but I was just a little girl who wanted to go to school. My mother used to tell me that one day I would not have to work so hard and I would be able to go to school. My sister stayed with our neighbours while my mother and I went to work. I never noticed my mother's tears and pain

or my sister's cries for help. I only saw that I wanted to be
a child. My mother and father also sewed garments at
night after dinner while my sister and I trimmed threads.

Our parents would take us to the park at 11 at night after
sewing, where we would play and eat yiros. Some nights
the neighbourhood children would play out the front of
restaurants under our apartment amongst the parked trucks.
I can still smell lamb yiros and chestnuts burning in the winter
nights. We would play until late. These nights are some of my
favourite childhood memories, despite all the hardships.

There were not many Bengalis, so we mostly spoke
Greek and were home-schooled by our father.
During the night, my sister was too scared to sleep,
so we held a string together to go to sleep.

East Pakistan became Bangladesh after the war in 1971.
Families in Bangladesh advised my dad not to return, as
Bangladesh was not a good place to raise children.

My family emigrated from Greece to Australia
in 1974 with only one suitcase each.

My dad was the inaugural curator of the Flinders
University Art Museum and my mum worked as a
dressmaker after arriving in Australia. Throughout their
life, before their retirement, they sewed garments every
night after dinner to pay their large mortgage.

My sister and I went to school shortly after arriving in Australia.
We started primary school at the end of 1974. We were, again,
in a new country with a new language, a new lifestyle and new
challenges. My parents tried to give us whatever they could.

I had lots of trouble with English at school, but I was very
good at math because of my home-schooling lessons with
my dad. I completed high school in 1980. I have always
worked part-time to assist my parents financially during my

school and university life. My high school years were filled with lots of love, laughter, tears, anger and frustration; life was full of challenges. Life was very hard, but I had a few beautiful friends that made my life bearable. My friends were from different countries, races, colour and religions. We, as friends, did not see the differences between us.

In the beginning, my parents were more tolerant and understanding. My parents were not strict with religion when we were in Greece. We celebrated Christmas, Easter, Chinese New Year, Eid al Fitr and Eid al Adha. However, they changed after arriving in Australia. Suddenly, my parents, who were Muslims, imposed religious beliefs on us and were blinded by their friends' advice. I found it hard to accept these changes. I felt like a lost sheep wandering around the desert. I was proud to be me, and I believed that I should have choices in life and not just follow life blindly.

My memories of these time are a mixture of happiness, loneliness, anger, frustration, confusion, and fear. Some of the memories I cherish are from the time my parents used to take us camping with our family friends. We used to go during long weekends and school holidays. At the camp site, the men played cards and the women sat by the stove and cooked five course meals for all of us. These women never seemed to complain, they just made sure their children were looked after and their men were happy. All of us children, we played on the lawn or by the lakes until late at night. We played our share of board and cards games.

I learned how to fish, put up a tent and play card games from my parents. We had lots of fun and lots of arguments. There were many fights between myself, my sister and our parents over our studies, friends, religion, and relationships. I was very lonely and felt that my vision was clouded by confusion and hurt. I found solace in my Nani's (maternal grandmother's) letters from Bangladesh. I feel that my Nani has never left me, even after she passed away. She is always in my heart.

I graduated from Flinders University in 1984. I had amazing friends at university too and they are still with me today;

My parents : Firoza and Amzad

My in laws: Rafaella and Cosimo

they are like my sisters. My university friends are always by my side and went through their own hardships; they all have stories to tell. University was an adventure, like the wave splashing against the white sand. I almost failed my first year of university, but my mum would not allow me to quit and told me that women in our family do not fail. She said, 'If you rub a rock again and again you will bend it, so go and try again', so I did. I ended up studying a Bachelor of Science with a major in hydrology.

Instead of doing honours in science and working for the CSIRO, I took a job at a data processing company in Adelaide. While working for this company, I met my future husband David, an Australian-born Italian. David worked in Balfours as an IT graduate. His office was close to mine. After 4 years of friendship, David and I were married in 1988. For people who believe in soul mates – David is my soul mate. Believe me, it was not an easy ride.

Before I met David, my parents had organised for me to marry a man from Bangladesh and, after exchanging letters with him, I agreed. The wedding was organised, the date was set, and the flowers ordered.

However, at the last minute, my family turned against the marriage because my fiancé did not like Adelaide and wanted to go back to Bangladesh. He asked me if I wanted to go back with him, but I could not; I felt like I did not belong anywhere at that time.

My father did not like the man he picked for me in the end. My father asked me if I wanted to marry this man, and I told him no, so my father sent him back. Then my parents sent me to Sydney and overseas to find a husband. If you were not married by 26 years old, you were considered to be an old maid or a slut. However, after many wedding proposals, no one was good enough for me according to my father. He did not allow me to marry anyone. I was brought up to respect my parents' wishes, so I obeyed them.

My life at that time became a clutter of mess again; I was floating between cultures, race, religion, hell and heaven, and I felt like no one really understood me. My Nani and David (my friend) were the only people who really understood me. I wanted to run away from this life, and I was suffocating, struggling for air, not knowing how to swim. I needed my Nani, so I flew to her.

The first time I went to Bangladesh to see my Nani was in 1986, then again 1987. Before leaving for a second trip to Bangladesh, I told David that if this time my Nani found a suitable match, I would marry the man she chose. So what did David do? David travelled to Bangladesh to meet my Nani; no man had ever done something like that for me. My Nani liked him. We had our first Nikka (Islamic wedding) in Bangladesh in front of my Nani. I was the eldest granddaughter and she wanted to see me as a bride. One of my maternal aunty had told me at that time that they had contacted my dad and received my parents' blessing,

Azmiri and Afroz

but later I discovered that this was untrue. My parents were terribly upset. We did not have mobile phones in those days.

David was also going through a very rough patch in his life and we felt that God wanted us to be together. We rescued each other in a world where we did not belong.

After returning to Australia, David went to ask my father for my hand in marriage – he was rejected, because in my father's eyes we were already married. He believed that if we were already married then we did not need his approval. My father felt disrespected by us. David and I were married again in Australia. My father did not come to the wedding; he broke my heart. He did not go to my sister's wedding when she married a Greek man, too. He broke my sister's heart. But all our lives, my mother stood by my sister and me. My mother has never given up on us. Even if it means that she still tries to tell us what to do with our lives.

David and I had many difficulties after we were married. Most of our families took us into their hearts because they did not want to lose us, but not my father or David's mother. It took my father and my mother-in-law a long time to accept us. It took us a long time to win their love and respect but we did. We have never given up on us. People fear what they do not know, so I understand why they were hesitant to accept us. Even though people have different religions, they are remarkably similar. People are blinded by their faith. I believe that all humankind has been created by our creator. Our creator cannot love one child more than the other, just like a mother. We are all part of the same rug.

There were many challenges that came with being married to a man from a different culture and religion, but God never left our side and we fought to keep our love alive. It was hard, extremely hard. Life never goes as smoothly as you plan. Be prepared to fight, jump, change, or go with the wind. Nobody really cares for anyone but themselves. Took me a long time to figure that out.

To save our marriage, we moved to Darwin in 1991 with our daughters Nadine and Jasmin, who were two and a half years and five months old respectively. There were pressures from our families to do things against our wishes and it was causing frictions between David and I. We had two more daughters in Darwin – Selina and Alicia.

Our six years in Darwin were good; we had wonderful friends and learnt a lot. Our friends became our families. The kindness I experienced in Darwin was amazing. While I was pregnant with Selina, I was sick most of the time, but angels in human form – our friends – looked after us. We had an outside fridge and it was always filled with milk, fish, bread, and home-cooked meals. The same friends took my girls to school and brought them home. I never had chance to miss our families in Adelaide.

After six years in Darwin, we moved back to Adelaide. I did not want to return, but I did it for my children and our parents. I wanted my children to have grandparents and experience their love, just like I did. I wanted them to have families who loved them. Our parents were getting old and we wanted to be here for them.

After returning to Adelaide my life really fell apart; I experienced post-natal depression and other health issues. Some days I did not want to wake up, but I had to take care of my daughters. Some days I felt like driving my daughters and I off a bridge, but I fought this battle with a brave face. I was reminded repeatedly that it was my battle and that I was strong enough to fight. I fought and I survived. My daughters gave me the strength to go on. Their laughter rang in my ears like a melody from heaven. They kept me sane. They are my little world.

You think my troubles stopped there and I lived happily ever after. I do not think so. Our Alicia was born hearing impaired and with an intellectual disability. The specialist told us that she would not speak and would have difficulty walking. After 21 years of therapy and medical appointments, homework, sleepless nights, tears, anger, feeling helpless, my daughter can walk and speak. I learned from Alicia how to love and accept, and I became a better human being.

Alicia had able friends, but they left Alicia behind as they grew up. Alicia did not get invited to their parties and if they did invite her, she sat in a corner the whole time. I felt lonely and sad for Alicia. I wanted to help her, so I tried to seek out support for her. It was a constant struggle and forever a battle ground. Only a parent of a child with a disability can understand what I've felt and experienced. I am still fighting for Alicia. Sometimes, I feel that I could not even die and leave Alicia behind.

Alicia joined sports clubs, like Special Olympics SA (sport clubs for athletes with intellectual disabilities), ARKS (swimming club for swimmers with disabilities) and netball clubs (for those with special needs). Alicia joined these clubs so that she could make friends and learn to understand group sports and their rules. Alicia excelled in swimming. She represented Australia at the World Special Olympics in Abu Dhabi in 2019. Alicia won a gold, a silver and two bronze medals for Australia.

I was there in Abu Dhabi with David to watch the world games. I saw the athletes with all abilities from 200 countries participating in their chosen sports. From these athletes I learned about tolerance, peace, understanding, empathy, kindness, love and most of all determination. These athletes were accepting of all. They didn't see race, colour, religion or ability. They cheered for all and gave a helping hand to anyone who needed it. I feel that the world leaders could learn something from these athletes.

A doctor advised us to take Alicia to childcare when she was three years old so she could socialise, and that is how my career began. I used to stay back at the childcare centre with Alicia and help. Eventually, they offered me job. It was difficult to go back to work after 16 years. I felt like an idiot; I could not speak or write properly and could only talk baby talk. I enrolled at TAFE to obtain a diploma in childcare, and I could not have completed it without the help of my husband and daughters.

I babysat other people's children for many years for extra money so that my girls could have things and do extracurricular activities. I wanted to give them opportunities. I did family day care for over 10 years. I worked for five years at the childcare centre, until I applied for a job with the government as a youth worker. I have been working for the government in child protection for the last 16 years.

However, Alicia's problems caused me to lose time with my other daughters. I spent 60 percent of my time with Alicia. I feel guilty, sad and unsure about my parenting with my older three daughters when they were growing up. All I know is that I did my best under the circumstances; I cooked for them, washed their clothes, took them to extracurricular activities, and made their home. I love them unconditionally.

Not all my memories from Adelaide are bad. My sister Azi, who went through some very hard times in her own life, was always there for me with her unconditional love. We shared good times and bad and that made us stronger in life.

My sister-in-law Toni (David's sister) and her family are my second family, and Toni is like a big sister to me.

I also had my friend Jackie, her husband Vince and their three beautiful daughters – they are my chosen family. We have seven daughters between us. Our two families had lots of fun together, fishing and camping year after year. These seven young girls were brave, fun and bright like sunshine; then, one day they were all grown up. I am so proud of them all.

My father, father-in-law, and my strong and courageous mother looked after me, advised me and gave me strength. I lost my dad and mother-in-law to dementia and my father-in-law to a blood clot in his lung. I miss them all (RIP). My

Vince and Jackie

Toni and Erminio

mother is still by our side. I am watching her grow older every day and I am dreading the day that she too will leave us. She has given us so much. She fulfilled our father's dream and took me and my sister to Bangladesh in February 2020, just before the coronavirus lockdown. My second daughter Jasmin and my sister's youngest son Gabriel came with us. It was an experience to remember. It was the first time I had been back to Bangladesh in 33 years and the last piece of my puzzle was added to my picture. My life made more sense now, I know who I am and where I am going. We went to Dhaka, Pabna to see where I was born and to see our first house, and we also went to Bhagalpur, my dad's village. We met uncles (chachas), the aunties (khalas, chachis), cousins and relatives – some people I knew and some I didn't.

The feelings I had didn't really make sense. I felt as though we were the same two little girls when we left Bangladesh in 1970, except our father was not there. The houses were different, they were more modern with modern technology, but everything else was the same.

The smell of the ground and the air was the same. The trees I saw the last time I was in Bangladesh were still there. The chickens were running around the house, the cows were chewing the hay, little vegetable gardens in people's yard, bare-feet children playing with smile on their faces – they are all still there. Except our grandparents. And we were not those little children playing. This is where I was born, this is where my story began.

It was good to be away for holidays, but it was great to be back home. Yes, I call Australia my home, it is where I have lived the longest. My husband, daughters, grandchildren, sons-in-laws, parents' parent-in laws, sister, sister-in-law, brother-in-law, nieces, nephews, cousins, aunties, uncles, relatives, and friends from Australia and overseas are in my world. These are my family.

David and Afroz

My husband and my daughters are the air that I breath. They are my life and they have always given me the strength to face any challenge. My daughters are my greatest achievements. I am proud of the wonderful women that they have become. My beautiful grandchildren are my lights, they are the ray of sunshine.

Nadine is a lawyer, married to Matt and live in Kuala Lumpur with their children Aston and Eva. Selina and her partner Andreas work for the federal government and live in Canberra.

Jasmin is a marine biologist with a doctorate, working at the University of South Australia. Alicia lives with David and I, works for Phoenix Bedford (supported employment) and swims and plays netball for the Special Olympics.

I have missed my children, grandchildren, family and friends during this coronavirus lockdown. This is my new challenge for now. Isolation has given me the chance to put together this book. I wanted to share a part of me with my family, friends and other people. I am sure I am not the only migrant and person to experience these challenges in life.

I just wanted to tell you that you are not the only one and you will not be the last. Do not give up in life because someone once told me that there is always a light at the end of the tunnel.

I keep busy in my life and I try to practice little acts of kindness every day. If I can make a difference for just one person in my life, then I will know that I have played my part in this world.

Life is not always perfect, but it is beautiful, and we must go with the flow.

Love you all,

Afroz

www.ingramcontent.com/pod-product-compliance
Ingram Content Group UK Ltd.
Pitfield, Milton Keynes, MK11 3LW, UK
UKHW022119230426
12048UKWH00010BA/598